COUNTRY INSIGHTS

CZECH REPUBLIC

Rob Humphreys

HODDER
Wayland

an imprint of Hodder Children's Books

COUNTRY INSIGHTS

BRAZIL • CHINA • CZECH REPUBLIC • DENMARK • FRANCE INDIA • JAPAN • KENYA

For more information on this series and other Hodder Wayland titles, go to www.hodderwayland.co.uk

GUIDE TO THIS BOOK

As well as telling you about the whole of the Czech Republic, this book looks closely at the city of Brno and the village of Nížkov.

This city symbol will appear at the top of the page and information boxes each time the book looks at Brno.

This rural symbol will appear each time the book looks at Nížkov.

Cover photograph: A Czech girl at school.

Title page: Gabriela, Šárka and Zdeněk at their home in Nížkov.

Contents page: Hrad Castle looks down over Prague, the capital of the Czech Republic.

Book editor: Louise Woods
Series editor: Polly Goodman
Book designer: Mark Whitchurch
Series designer: Tim Mayer
Consultant: Anne Marley, Principal Librarian, Children and Schools' Library Service for Hampshire.

First published in 1997 by Wayland Publishers Ltd

Revised and updated in 2006 by Hodder Wayland, an imprint of Hodder Children's Books

© Copyright 1997 Hodder Wayland

British Library Cataloguing in Publication Data
Humphreys, Rob
  Czech Republic. – (Country Insights)
  1. City and town life – Czech Republic – Juvenile literature
  2. Country life – Czech Republic – Juvenile literature
  3. Czech Republic – Social conditions – Juvenile literature
  I. Title
  943.7'105

ISBN-10: 0750248203
ISBN-13: 9780750248204

Typeset by Mark Whitchurch, England
Printed in China

Picture Acknowledgements: All photographs by Dorian Shaw of Axiom Photographic Agency, except the following: Cover: Corbis; page 11 (top): Image Bank; page 13 (bottom): Robert Harding Picture Library.
All map artwork by Hardlines.
Border Artwork by Kate Davenport.

Hodder Children's Books
A division of Hodder Headline Limited
338 Euston Road, London NW1 3BH

Contents

The Czech Republic

The Czech Republic is a small, land-locked country at the centre of Europe. It is divided into two main provinces: Bohemia, to the west, and Moravia, to the east. The capital, Prague, lies at the centre of Bohemia, on the banks of the Vltava river.

The Czechs are a Slav people, whose ancestors settled in central and eastern Europe over 1,500 years ago. For many hundreds of years, the country was ruled over by the Austrian royal family. In 1918, the Czechs, along with their neighbours, the Slovaks, formed a new republic called Czechoslovakia. In 1948, a communist government took over Czechoslovakia and the Czechs lost control over their own affairs. Communist rule lasted until 1989, and the country became very poor during this time.

◀ *This view over Prague shows the white church of St Vavřinec in the foreground.*

The Czech Republic's place in the world

N

This book will ▶ take you to the city of Brno and the village of Nížkov. You can find these places on the map.

0   100 km

0   50 miles

CZECH REPUBLIC FACTS

Total land area:	78,866 km²
Population:	10.3 million
Language:	Czech
Capital city:	Prague
Highest mountain:	Sněžka, 1,602 m
Currency:	Česká koruna

There have been great changes in the country since communism collapsed, in 1989. For the first time in many years, Czechs can now travel abroad freely, start their own private businesses, and choose their own government.

In 1993, Czechoslovakia split into two separate countries: the Czech Republic and Slovakia. Today, the Czech Republic is one of the richest and most successful of the old communist countries.

Charles Bridge, a fourteenth-century ▶ bridge across the Vltava river, in Prague, was built long before the age of the motor vehicle. Now it is a fashionable tourist attraction as well as a route for people on their way to work.

The city of Brno

Brno is the second-largest city in the Czech Republic. Its name is pronounced 'Br-no' – the 'o' is short as in the word 'hot'. The city lies in the south-east of the country and is the capital of the province of Moravia.

Only 200 years ago, Brno was still a small town with about 20,000 people, mainly living inside the old city walls. The town's landmark has always been the cathedral, with its needle-thin spires.

BRNO FACTS	
Population:	369,229
Height above sea-level:	223 m

▼ **Behind the spire of the church of St Jakub, you can just see the high-rise flats of Brno's suburbs in the far distance.**

The old medieval walls were taken down in 1860 and replaced by parks, gardens and a ring road. At that time, Brno quickly began to grow into a big, industrial city, surrounded by textile and engineering factories.

▲ *Shopping at the vegetable market in the old town.*

In the 1960s and 1970s, Brno grew much larger, with lots of high-rise housing built in the new suburbs of the city. These blocks of flats are the first things you see as you enter the city. The old town is still in the city centre, with many cobbled streets and squares, and several old churches. Only taxis and trams are allowed to drive around the central streets of the old town. This is where most people do their shopping, and the vegetable market, held in one of the old town squares, is very popular.

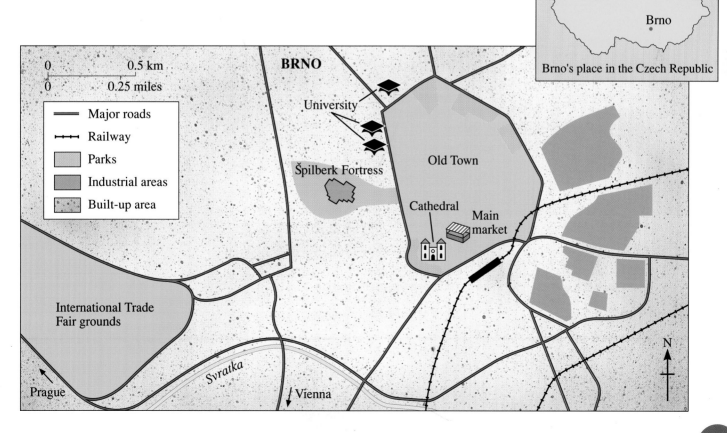

The village of Nížkov

Nížkov, pronounced 'Neeshkoff', is a small farming village in the uplands of the Czech Republic, which stretch across the middle of the country from north to south. These gently rolling hills, known as the *vrchovina*, form the border between the two regions of Bohemia and Moravia. Over the last 100 years, all the traditional wooden houses in Nížkov have been replaced by brick and stone buildings. The oldest building in the village is the church, which was built over 700 years ago. The village also has a post office, a school, a pub and three shops. The nearest railway station is 3 km away on the main line from Brno to Prague, but only local trains stop there. There is no petrol station, and although almost every family has a car, most people walk, cycle or use the bus to get around.

NÍŽKOV FACTS

Population of Nížkov and surrounding area:	805
Height above sea-level:	526 m

▼ **The church of Nížkov, with its dome-shaped spire, is the highest point in the village. All the houses cluster below it.**

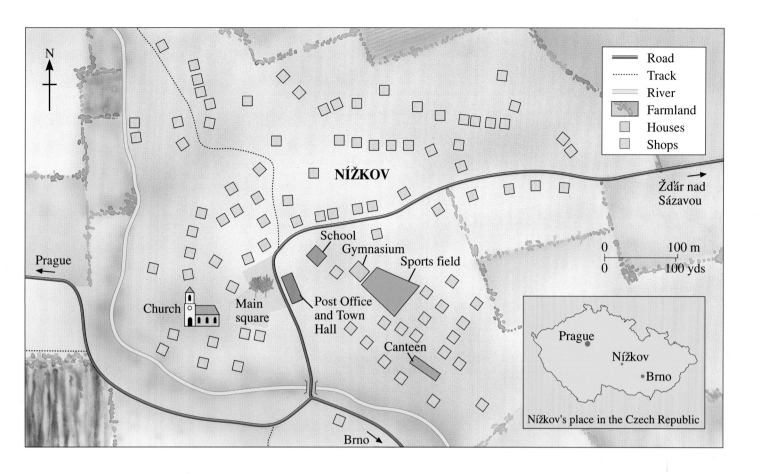

Unlike Brno, Nížkov has changed very little over the last fifty years. Roughly the same number of people live here, and farming is still the main activity. Although some young people leave to look for jobs in the neighbouring towns or in other parts of the country, enough stay to prevent the population from dropping.

The streets of ▶ Nížkov are quiet and safe for these children to play in after school.

Land and climate

Two-thirds of the Czech Republic is forested, mostly with spruce, but also with pine and beech trees. Mountains form most of the country's natural borders. In 1945, after Germany had lost the Second World War, the 3 million German-speakers who lived in the border regions were driven out of the country. Even today, not many people live in these areas. Most Czechs live in the towns and cities in the flatter valleys of the Odra, Morava and Elbe rivers.

The Czech Republic has four seasons. Winters, which last from November to March, are cold. Easterly winds from Siberia force the temperature well below freezing, and there are often heavy snowfalls in the hills and mountains.

▼ *Cows grazing in the rolling hills of north Bohemia.*

Summers are hot, especially on the flat plains of the Morava and Elbe rivers, with temperatures sometimes reaching 30 °C. Spring and autumn are shorter seasons, with more moderate temperatures.

▲ *Skiing in the mountains of north Moravia.*

The country has a lot of coal underground: brown coal (lignite) in north Bohemia, and black coal in north Moravia. Coal is the main source of energy, though the country also depends heavily on oil and gas imported from Russia. Acid rain is caused by pollution from the coal-fired power stations, and this rain has badly damaged the country's forests. The Czech Republic has one nuclear power station, in Moravia. It also generates some hydroelectricity from the dams on the Vltava river.

AVERAGE DAILY TEMPERATURE IN PRAGUE		
Winter (Jan):	Minimum:	−5°C
	Maximum:	0°C
Summer (July):	Minimum:	14°C
	Maximum:	25°C

▼ *These thick pine forests are in the north, on the border with Poland.*

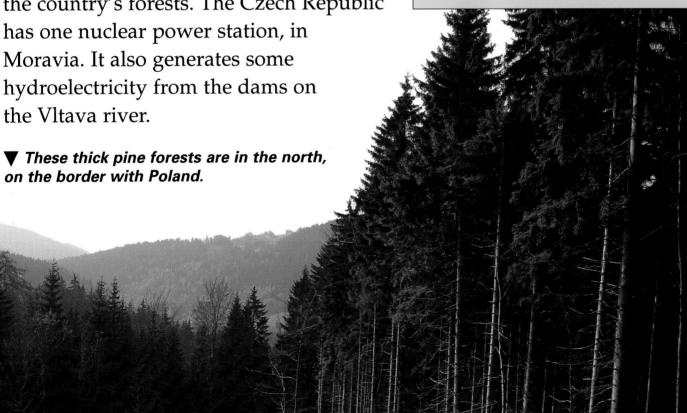

Brno's land and climate

Brno lies on the border between the hilly uplands to the north-west, and the flat plains to the south-east. The city centre is built around two hills. The Gothic cathedral of Saint Peter and Saint Paul sits on the smaller hill, and the Špilberk fortress occupies the taller hill. On a clear day, you can see as far as the hills around Mikulov, a town 50 km to the south, near the Austrian border.

Many of the city's new suburbs were once small villages in their own right, which have since been swallowed up by the city. The outer suburbs in the north and west of the city have forests and hills on their doorstep. They are all within easy reach of the city centre by tram or bus.

▼ *If you stand on the hill by the Špilberk fortress, this is the view of Brno that you see.*

Although winters in Brno are cold and often bring snow, the summer is hot with plenty of sunshine. The flat plains to the south of the city are especially good for growing fruits such as cherries, apricots and grapes. Most of the country's wine is produced in the vineyards to the south of Brno.

Just beyond the city limits to the north, is the Moravian karst region. Karst landscapes are made of limestone that has been worn away by rainwater to form underground rivers, lakes and caves. The karst region is one of the most popular tourist attractions in Moravia.

▲ Collecting conkers from one of the city's many parks in autumn.

You can take a boat ride to explore these ▶ *underground caves, which are in the karst region just north of Brno.*

Nížkov's land and climate

Nížkov lies on a small tributary of the Sázava river, which flows west into the Vltava river, just south of Prague. In the uplands around Nížkov, the climate is generally much cooler than in Brno. The cherry, apple and rowan trees, which line the country roads, come into blossom slightly later here. In winter, the snows are much deeper and the temperature can drop to as low as –25 °C. Children in Nížkov learn to ski from a very early age, as this is often the best way to get around in the winter.

▲ *A map of Nížkov and the surrounding villages, made by schoolchildren from the village.*

▼ *Autumn leaves fall earlier in Nížkov than in Brno, because the village is on higher land.*

The uplands have always been one of the Czech Republic's poorest regions. The soil is not very fertile and is only really good for growing potatoes and barley. Wheat and rye are grown, but the quality is poor. Smaller quantities of other crops are also grown on the local farms, including rape seed, peas, oats, beetroot, caraway seeds, and maize, which can be made into feed for animals. Villagers fish for carp in the nearby freshwater ponds.

It rains most in June, July and August. August marks the beginning of the harvest, the busiest time of the year for any farming community. Just about everyone, young and old, lends a hand in the fields during this season.

'I like the farming life, especially the fresh air, the smell of the fruit, the meadows in blossom and the birds.' – Bohuslav Hais, farmer (below).

◄ Bohuslav Hais prepares cabbage before it is put into the village shop to be sold.

Home life

Family life is very important in the Czech Republic, and several generations often live together. Most Czech families have two children. Grandparents often look after the children while their parents are at work.

Czech homes vary greatly. In some parts of the countryside, people still live in traditional, timber-framed houses, while in town and city suburbs, there are modern, high-rise blocks of flats, called *paneláky* (meaning prefabricated).

▲ *This big farmhouse in the countryside outside Brno is occupied by just one family.*

◀ Paneláky, *like this one, house hundreds of families in the Czech Republic.*

◀ *A typical Czech kitchen, with a gas oven for cooking.*

FAVOURITE FOODS

Smažený sýr
(pronounced 'Smadjeny-seer')
A thick slice of Czech cheese, deep-fried in batter and served with potatoes and tartare sauce.

Palačinky
(pronounced 'Pala-chinky')
This is most Czech children's favourite dessert – pancakes filled with fruit, or chocolate and cream.

Párek
A type of hot dog: a boiled sausage served with mustard and a white roll.

To save space, many Czech homes have special beds that can be turned into sofas during the day. Czechs usually take their shoes off when they go indoors and put on slippers known as *pantofle*. Visitors are also expected to take off their shoes, and are given *pantofle* to wear by the family.

Most Czechs eat their main meal of the day at lunchtime. Lunch usually begins with soup, followed by a main course of meat with potatoes or dumplings. Czech dumplings are made with flour and milk and then cut into thick slices, rather like bread.

In the evening, the meal usually consists of cold meats, cheese and bread, served with tea or coffee. It is really more of a snack, followed by chocolate, biscuits or an apple. Many Czechs have a sweet tooth, and enjoy cakes and ice-cream at any time of the day.

Home life in Brno

In Brno, as in all big towns, people live in many types of houses and flats, from high-rise *paneláky* to luxury villas. The *paneláky* are mainly in the city's outer suburbs, and have been built over the last fifty years. Although these flats have central heating and modern fittings, many of them were badly built and they often need repairing.

In the inner suburbs, there are two- or three-storey villas, some with their own gardens. Many of these used to belong to rich Germans before the end of the Second World War.

In 1948, these and all but the smallest of other houses were divided

▲ *A Czech mother reads a story to her children at bedtime.*

◄ *Most people in Brno live in flats. Very few have their own garden.*

into flats after the communists took over the country. As a result, most people in Brno live in flats, with one or two bedrooms, a kitchen, a bathroom and a living room. Many blocks of flats have a central courtyard with balconies looking down on to them. In good weather, neighbours sit outside and chat.

Most homes in Brno and other Czech cities have hot water and central heating, and most have a television set and a washing machine. Computers, videos, stereos and other high-tech gadgets are becoming more common in Czech homes, too.

There are lots of different places to buy food in Brno, and most people don't have far to go to get to their nearest shop. Apart from the popular vegetable market in the city centre, there are also various supermarkets and smaller food stores around the city and its suburbs.

'We like getting take-away food some evenings, instead of having to cook.'
– Andrea and Tomáš, students at Brno University.

Home life in Nížkov

◀ Karel Novotný's, single-storey house, which he built in the centre of Nížkov for his family.

There are no *paneláky* in Nížkov, and few houses compared to Brno. Most families own their own house, which is usually built on one or two floors and surrounded by a small plot of land. Villagers use this to grow their own vegetables and keep a few hens and geese.

▲ The Novotný family relax in the evening and talk about the events of the day.

Nížkov is a very quiet village where everyone knows everybody else. Apart from the tractors from the local farms, traffic is very light, since most people do not use their cars much during the week. There is a regular bus service to the nearest big town, Žďár nad Sázavou, which is 12 km away.

Karel Novotný is a lorry driver, and lives with his wife and three children. He delivers frozen meat and vegetables from Nížkov to shops all over the Czech Republic. His wife, Jana, has a part-time job delivering newspapers. She finishes work in time to look after the children after school and to make the evening meal. Jana's ten-year-old daughter, Šárka, helps her mother to clear up, wash the dishes and do the shopping.

Jana's parents also live in Nížkov. Her father used to work at the engineering factory in Žďár nad Sázavou. He retired ten years ago, and now he gets a state pension. Jana's mother still works part-time as a teacher in the village school.

▼ *The evening meal is often the only time the whole family eat together.*

Work

For over 100 years, the Czechs have relied on heavy industries such as steel, coal and manufacturing. The country has exported trains, cars, and more recently, nuclear reactors to the rest of Europe. It has also equipped their armies. Since 1989, however, these old-fashioned heavy industries have found it difficult to keep up with the rest of Europe. The working people are well educated and highly skilled, but the technology used in the country is out of date. Many factories have had to lay off workers and cut down production. Others have had to close down completely.

▼ **This fertilizer factory will need to bring its technology up to date in order to survive.**

Under the communists, everyone was guaranteed a job for life – in fact, it was against the law not to have a job. Unemployment came as a shock to many Czechs.

TYPE OF WORK		
		Percentage of working population
Industry		39
Services		57
Agriculture		4

Luckily, most of those who were unemployed have now found jobs in the thousands of new companies which have started up since 1989.

Now that it is a lot easier to visit the Czech Republic, tourism has become one of the country's most important industries, especially in Prague. In 2004, nearly 8 million tourists visited the country. This has created many new jobs for people who want to work in hotels and restaurants. There are also new jobs making consumer goods, such as televisions and CD-players. Other people work in computer technology, advertising, and the leisure and service industries.

▼ *This woman works as a hotel receptionist. She has to be able to speak German and English, as well as Czech.*

Work in Brno

Brno is a centre for textiles and engineering. It is also the agricultural centre for south Moravia, where most of the country's wine is produced.

The city's international trade fairs are very important in central Europe, and business people from all over the world go to them. The biggest one is the International Engineering Trade Fair, which takes place every year in September. There are other fairs throughout the year. Lots of people come to these fairs, which usually last for a few days. This provides good business for the city's hotels, shops and restaurants, too.

▼ *A businessman makes arrangements to attend an important trade fair in Brno.*

▼ **Brno was one of the first Czech cities to get a new fleet of modern trams.**

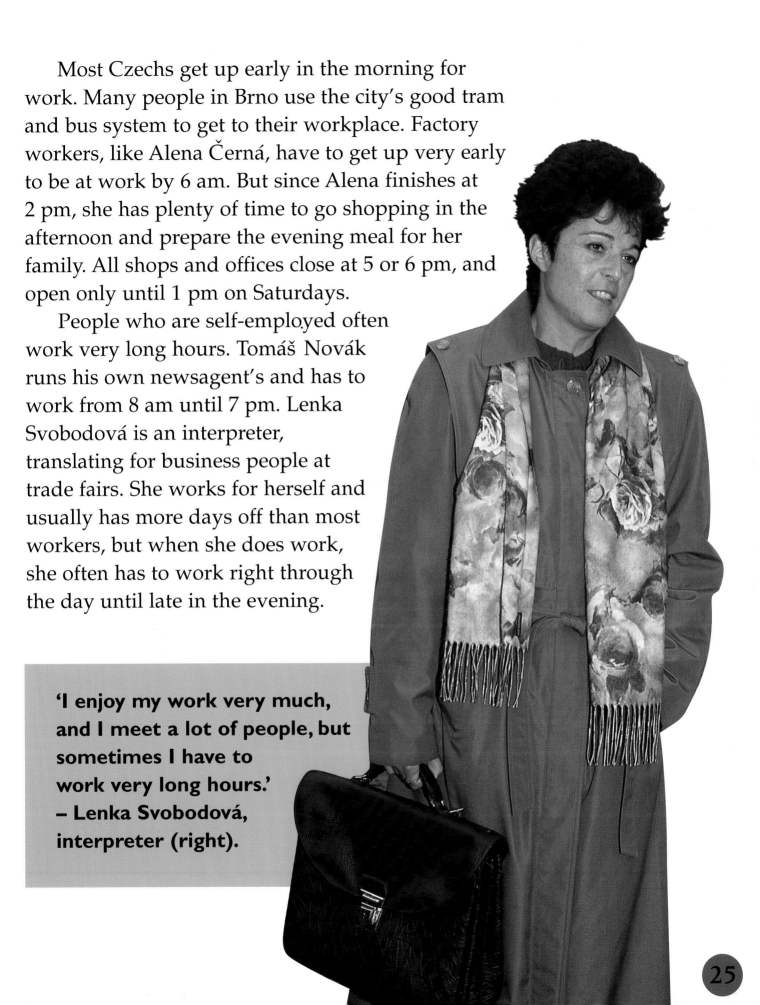

Most Czechs get up early in the morning for work. Many people in Brno use the city's good tram and bus system to get to their workplace. Factory workers, like Alena Černá, have to get up very early to be at work by 6 am. But since Alena finishes at 2 pm, she has plenty of time to go shopping in the afternoon and prepare the evening meal for her family. All shops and offices close at 5 or 6 pm, and open only until 1 pm on Saturdays.

People who are self-employed often work very long hours. Tomáš Novák runs his own newsagent's and has to work from 8 am until 7 pm. Lenka Svobodová is an interpreter, translating for business people at trade fairs. She works for herself and usually has more days off than most workers, but when she does work, she often has to work right through the day until late in the evening.

'I enjoy my work very much, and I meet a lot of people, but sometimes I have to work very long hours.' – Lenka Svobodová, interpreter (right).

Work in Nížkov

Throughout the communist period, most villagers in Nížkov worked in the area's big co-operative farm. Wages were low, but workers were paid all year round and were secure in their jobs. After 1989, the co-operative farm was divided up into much smaller private farms. Many of these farms are now run by single families, who can only take on extra workers at harvest time.

Ladislav and Zdena Pospíšil run their farm on their own for most of the year.

Ladislav and Zdena Pospíšil, who are both in their fifties, are typical local farmers. Their children have chosen not to follow the family tradition of farming, but they help out during harvest time. Ladislav and Zdena get up at 4 am to feed the cattle, and work in the fields until it gets dark. They also keep rabbits, hens, ducks, geese and pigs.

'The busiest time for all farmers is from June until early November. We work up to 14 hours a day, unless it rains very hard.' – Ladislav Pospíšil, farmer.

Some people work in the village's three shops, in the school or in the post office. Several new businesses have started up since 1989. The largest one is a construction company, which employs a lot of workers who build and decorate houses. Other new businesses in the village include a blacksmith's, a dressmaker's, a hairdresser's and a plumber's.

Some villagers have to travel to work in the nearby town of Žďár nad Sázavou, which has a large engineering factory that makes machine tools. Factory workers have to catch a bus from the village at 5 am to get to work by 6 am.

▲ **Workmen insulate a house to protect it from the cold and wet of winter. For the last five years, there has been plenty of building work in the village.**

▼ **At work in the village post office.**

Going to school

All Czech children between the ages of six and fifteen must go to school. Most begin nursery school at three or four years old. They then go on to basic school, or *základní škola*, at the age of six and stay there until they are fifteen. Each class has one teacher for all subjects in the first four or five years, then they have a different teacher for each subject. In the larger cities, there are schools which specialize in one subject, for example, science, languages, woodwork or sports.

Children are given school reports twice a year, at the end of January and at the end of June. There are also exams at the end of June. If a child fails to do well enough in any subject, he or she may have to repeat the whole year.

◄ **This boy is learning carpentry skills in a school that specializes in woodwork.**

▲ **A game of charades helps children in their English lesson at school.**

▲ *Games lessons in the afternoon are an important part of the school curriculum.*

Czech children do not have to wear school uniforms. However, all children (and their teachers) must wear *pantofle* inside the school building, just as they do at home. When they arrive at school in the morning, the children go straight to the cloakrooms to change out of their shoes and into their *pantofle*.

The atmosphere inside the school is very quiet, and there is not much noise in the school corridors. The children do not go out into the playground during break time, but they can play with their friends inside. Outdoor activities and games take place in the afternoon, after lessons finish.

SCHOOL HOLIDAYS

Autumn half-term:	2 days
Christmas:	2 weeks
Easter:	1 week
Summer:	2 months

29

School in Brno

Brno has plenty of schools from nursery level right through to university. Seventeen-year-old Václav Cerný goes to a senior high school, which specializes in subjects like history, literature and politics. He has to catch the tram to school at 7.30 am.

Václav's younger brother, ten-year-old Jan, goes to the basic school near their home. Like most pupils, Jan walks to school for 8 am, when lessons begin, carrying his books on his back in a brightly coloured school-bag.

'School's OK, but my favourite lesson is PE, when I get to play football and other games.' – Jan Cerný, aged 10.

Many children in Brno ▶ live close enough to their school to walk there.

Jan has five or six different lessons every day, with a short break after every lesson. Each lesson lasts for 45 minutes. Lunch is at 12.30 or 1.30 pm, depending on the day.

After lunch, the school organizes outdoor activities and games. Children do not have to go to these classes if they prefer not to. Václav and Jan both go on at least one school outing a month, to a museum, a theatre or some other event. There are nature trips, too. Every spring, there is a week-long school trip to the mountains of North Moravia. There are not enough places on these trips for all the children to go, so they must take turns.

▲ **Lunchtime in the school canteen. Children queue to be served with a hot meal.**

▼ *A game of 'Yes or No' in an English lesson, where the teacher says something in English, and the children race to the chair marked 'yes' or the chair marked 'no' depending on whether the statement was true or not.*

School in Nížkov

The main school in Nížkov is a basic school for children aged between six and fifteen. To go to senior high school, the children must travel to the nearby town of Žďár nad Sázavou. They catch the bus from Nížkov at 7 am. There is also a nursery school in Nížkov for children aged between three and six.

The basic school in Nížkov is quite small, with just 177 pupils and thirteen teachers. In Nížkov, school starts earlier than in Brno, at 7.15 am. Some children arrive even earlier and spend an hour in the school playgroup or *družina*. Like most children from Nížkov, Šárka Novotná walks to school by herself, or with her younger brother and sister.

▼ *These fifth-year children are learning English at school in Nížkov.*

All three Novotný children have to get up very early in the morning in order to get to school on time.

Šárka has her lunch break at midday. The meal is served in the village nursery school, five minutes' walk away. Šárka likes the food at school, except when it is spinach or soup.

The children are given a small amount of homework twice a week. Any children who do not do their homework are made to stay behind after school and do extra work. There are regular school outings to the cinema and theatre, and once a year the whole school goes on a day trip. Last year they went to the safari zoo.

▲ *Children talk about their news on their way to school in Nížkov.*

Šárka does her homework in her bedroom. ▼

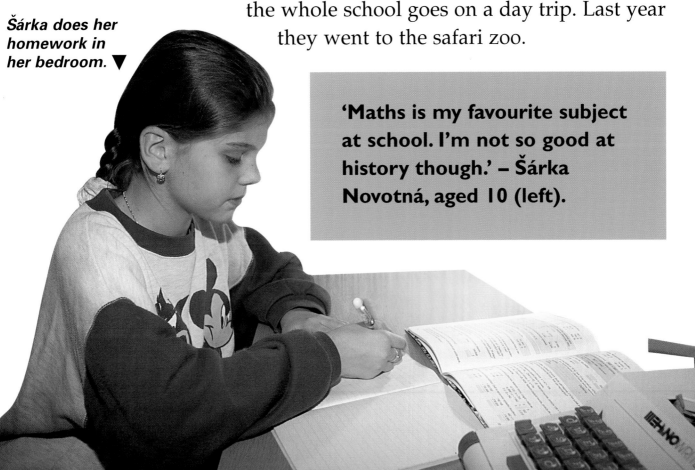

'Maths is my favourite subject at school. I'm not so good at history though.' – Šárka Novotná, aged 10 (left).

Leisure time

Ice hockey and football are the most popular sports in the Czech Republic. Even the smallest towns and villages have a football team, and most large towns have a *zimní stadión* ('winter stadium'), where people play ice hockey. Sometimes, younger children practise ice hockey outside, using roller skates instead of ice skates.

Many Czechs love to go walking and camping. There are marked paths all over the country, which make it easy for people to plan their walks. From an early age, many children go on organized summer camps, where they learn rock-climbing and canoeing. In the evenings, they often sit round the camp fire and sing popular folk songs, accompanied by the guitar.

Czechs are keen tourists at home and abroad. At weekends, many families visit a nearby castle or museum and have a picnic. Under the communists, very few Czechs were allowed to travel abroad for their holidays. Since 1989, however, coach tours to neighbouring countries have become very popular.

◀ *A walker plans his route in the Krkonoše national park.*

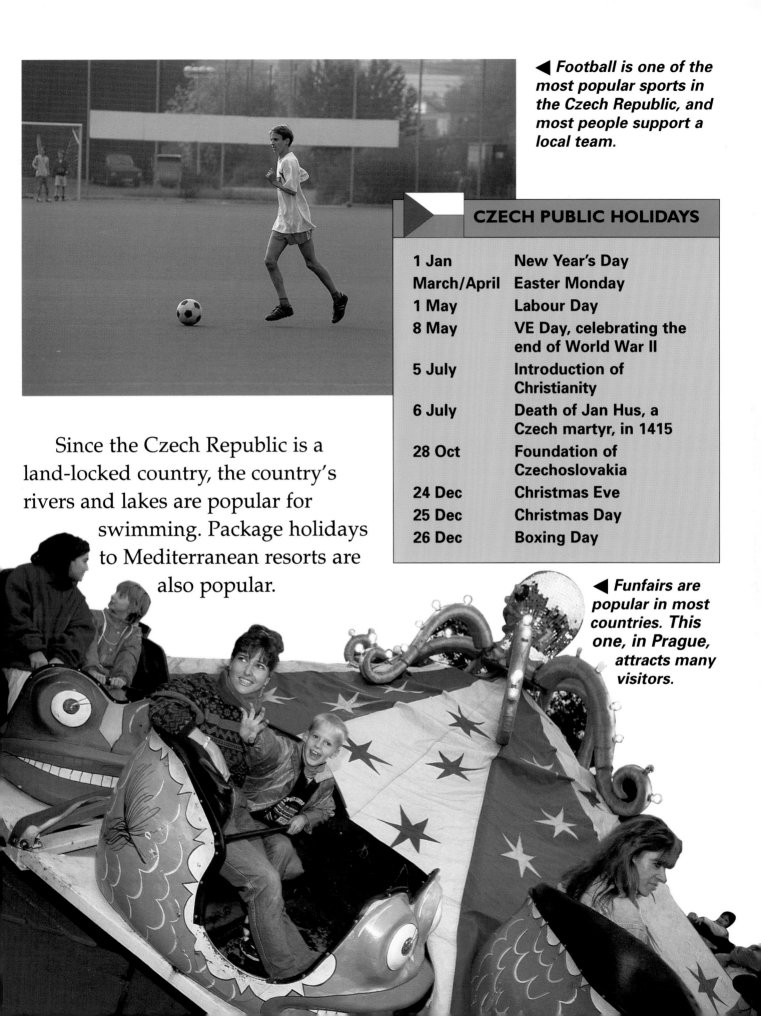

◀ Football is one of the most popular sports in the Czech Republic, and most people support a local team.

CZECH PUBLIC HOLIDAYS

1 Jan	New Year's Day
March/April	Easter Monday
1 May	Labour Day
8 May	VE Day, celebrating the end of World War II
5 July	Introduction of Christianity
6 July	Death of Jan Hus, a Czech martyr, in 1415
28 Oct	Foundation of Czechoslovakia
24 Dec	Christmas Eve
25 Dec	Christmas Day
26 Dec	Boxing Day

Since the Czech Republic is a land-locked country, the country's rivers and lakes are popular for swimming. Package holidays to Mediterranean resorts are also popular.

◀ Funfairs are popular in most countries. This one, in Prague, attracts many visitors.

Leisure time in Brno

Most families in Brno like to get out of the city at weekends. Many families own their own *chata*, or have friends who do. A *chata* can be anything from a small piece of land with a simple wooden hut on it, to a much larger country cottage. Here people from the cities can enjoy the cleaner country air, grow their own vegetables, or simply relax with friends. Even those people who do not have a *chata* to go to, usually head out into the countryside for the day if the weather is good. There are forests and hills to the north and west of Brno, just a short tram ride from the city centre.

▼ *Czech families who are lucky enough to have a* chata *can escape from the city at weekends.*

Children in Brno playing ▶ in the school gymnasium after school.

'We have a television at home, but I prefer to go out and do some sport with my friends after school.' – Eva Kriatková, aged 13.

▼ *Brno's new sports stadium, one of the city's popular leisure facilities.*

There are many more leisure facilities in Brno now than there were ten years ago. Next to the football and ice-hockey stadiums, there is now a new leisure complex. It has a multi-screen cinema, a gymnasium, snooker hall, ten-pin bowling alley and roller-skating rink. The city also has a Grand Prix circuit, which hosts an international motorcycling race every August.

Young people have several cinemas, discos and rock clubs to go to, though most international bands perform only in Prague. Older people sometimes prefer to go to the theatre or the opera house. Tickets are quite cheap, and people like to dress up smartly to go there.

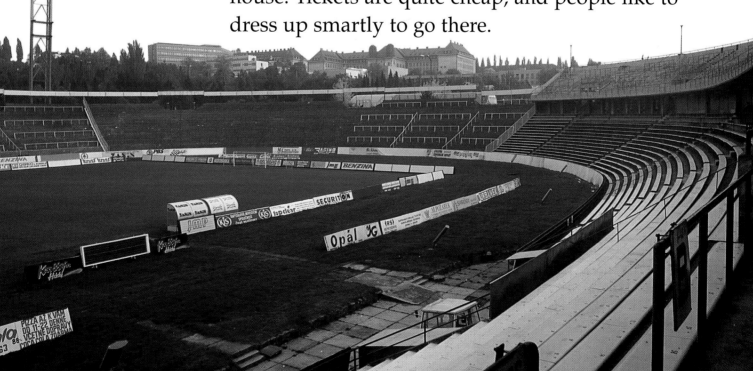

Leisure time in Nížkov

Life in Nížkov is much quieter than in Brno, and sometimes the only sound in the evening is the chiming of the village church clock. Every house in the village has a television, but many children prefer to spend their free time outside with their friends. After school, Šárka Novotná likes to play *prehazovaná*, a popular game similar to volleyball.

As farmers, Ladislav and Zdena Pospíšil do not have very much free time. Ladislav usually watches the television news in the evening, but once a week he goes to the local pub to drink beer and play cards. The pub serves hot food throughout the day.

People who want to visit a restaurant or see a film must drive or catch the bus to Žďár nad Sázavou.

Children in Nížkov have lots of opportunities to enjoy outdoor life. There are freshwater ponds nearby where they can go fishing. The hills surrounding Nížkov are good for walking, and in winter there is usually plenty of snow for skiing.

▼ *The church plays an important part in the life of Nížkov, but nowadays it is mainly the older generation who go there.*

'*Prehazovaná* is my favourite game, but I also like swimming in the summer'.
– Šárka Novotná, aged 10.

Skateboarding is ▼ popular even in small villages like Nižkov.

At Christmas, the focus is on children. On the evening of 5 December, three villagers disguise themselves as Saint Nicholas, the Devil and an angel. They call round at each house, threatening to give naughty children coal, before finally giving them presents for being good. On Christmas Eve, the children open presents from their family and friends. Carp is the traditional Christmas dish, taken fresh from the local fishponds and kept alive in the bath until it is cooked and eaten.

▼ *Nižkov schoolchildren have lots of opportunities for getting out into the countryside. These children are on a school outing.*

The future

The future for the Czech Republic is much better than it was under communist rule. Now the country is a democracy again, people are free to express their opinions, travel abroad, start their own businesses and to write and read what they like. None of these things were allowed under communist rule.

However, there is a lot of work to be done as the country adjusts to its new government. The Czech Republic needs help from other countries to bring its industry up to date, and to create jobs for the unemployed.

▼ *Tomáš Novák runs his own newspaper shop. He is now free to sell many different newspapers, which were not allowed under communist rule.*

The biggest problem facing the country is the pollution caused by the coal-fired power stations, which creates a permament smog over parts of the country, particularly North Bohemia. Nuclear power produces 31 per cent of the country's electricity, but some people think it is dangerous. The country needs to look for other sources of energy, such as solar power and wind power, which cause less pollution.

The Czech Republic can solve these problems in time. In fact, the country became a full member state of the European Union (EU) in May 2004, and this should help to address some of these issues.

▲ *Tourism is a growing industry in the Czech Republic. New hotels like this one will create wealth and employment.*

▼ *Smokestacks like these create a lot of pollution in Czech towns and cities.*

The future of Brno

More people can ▶ *afford cars these days, so there is much more traffic in Brno today than there was a few years ago. This often causes traffic jams and congestion.*

Brno's problems are typical of the country as a whole. It makes its money from heavy industries such as engineering. These industries are now producing less and employing fewer workers. Many big factories have been taken over by companies from Germany, Italy and the USA. This has stopped them from being closed down completely, so the number of people who have lost their jobs is much smaller than people feared. Although unemployment still threatens the region, as they grow, new businesses help to keep unemployment low by taking on more workers. There are new shops, cafés and restaurants all over the city centre.

'At one time it looked as though all the city's factories were going to close down. The fact that they are still in business at all is a success of sorts.'
– Alena Cerná, factory worker.

There is much more traffic in Brno today than in 1989. Although public transport is more expensive than it was, prices are still kept low with money from the government. This is to encourage people to use the trams and buses rather than their cars. Trains are improving, too, and you can now travel easily by train between Brno and Prague, Berlin and Vienna.

The city's trade fairs have gone from strength to strength since 1989, creating jobs for many people, and increasing business at the city's hotels, shops and restaurants. Brno's trade fairs have also allowed foreign business people to meet up with their Czech partners. Czechs have been very good at getting foreign companies to put money into the country, but Prague often gets the larger part of this new money.

▼ *Waiting at a tram stop. Cheap fares encourage people to use trams rather than cars, which cause less pollution.*

▼ *Foreign investors talk business at a Brno trade fair.*

The future of Nížkov

When the communist government was in power, the local co-operative farm employed most of the villagers in Nížkov. The government provided money to keep the farm going, and there was always work. There was always enough food, too, and life in the village did not change much over the years. However, the farming methods were not very up to date, and there was no reason for people to work more than was absolutely necessary.

Since 1989, many people have got back the land that the communists took from them. Farmers can now work for themselves and their families. They know that if they work hard, their farm will do well, and they will make more money.

▼ *Farmers like Ladislav Pospíšil have to work even harder than before, because they no longer get help from the government.*

The government no longer gives the farmers any money to help them, so life is much harder than before. But the village still has a strong sense of community, so people are happy to help each other through these difficult years of change.

Like most villages, Nížkov's biggest problem is trying to stop its young people from leaving. There is not much choice of work in the village and the farm work is usually seasonal. However, there is more opportunity now for starting up small businesses, and several are doing very well. There are also jobs at the nearby factory in Žďár nad Sázavou. This factory is doing well thanks to new orders from less economically developed countries, such as Pakistan.

▲ *This builder has become successful by starting up his own business in Nížkov. Small businesses will be very important to villagers in the future.*

'I think there is a better standard of living now than under the communists, with more choice in the shops and more opportunities for my children.' – Jana Novotná, villager.

The children of Nížkov will ▶ *have an easier life than their parents have had.*

Glossary

Acid rain Rain containing acid that kills trees and plants. This acid comes from waste from factories.

Ancestors People from whom we are descended.

Chata A Czech word for a small country cottage.

Communist government A type of government where everything is owned and controlled by the community for its own benefit, instead of being for the benefit of a few rich people. A communist government ruled Czechoslovakia from 1948 until 1989.

Co-operative A business run by the workers themselves, with everyone sharing the profits.

Democracy A system of government which lets people vote for any political party they want to.

Gothic A style of building popular from the twelfth to the sixteenth centuries, which featured pointed arches and tall spires.

Heavy industries Industries such as steel and engineering, which make large items such as machinery for factories and cars.

High-rise housing Tall blocks of flats that can house many families.

Hydroelectricity Electricity produced from the power of water.

Interpreter Someone who translates speech from one language to another.

Land-locked A country that has no coastline or access to the sea.

Medieval From the Middle Ages, AD 600-1500.

Prefabricated Buildings that have been put together using ready-made sections.

Provinces Regions of a country.

Republic A type of government without a king, queen, emperor or empress, usually ruled by an elected president and a parliament.

Ring road A road that goes around the outside of a town, to keep traffic out of the centre.

Self-employed A person who runs their own business.

Service industry Businesses such as tourism and banking, which do not make goods but instead supply people with services they need.

Slav A group of people who come from the central and eastern part of Europe.

Solar power Energy from the sun.

Suburbs Outer parts of a town or city where people live.

Trade fair A big meeting of business people where they can buy and sell their products.

Translating Changing a word or sentence from one language into another.

Tributary A river or stream that flows into a bigger river.

Uplands A mainly flat area on the top of a range of hills.

Further information

Books to read

The Changing Face of The Czech Republic
by Jacob Rihosek
(Hodder Wayland, 2004)

Picture a Country: Czech Republic
by Henry Pluckrose
(Franklin Watts, 2001)

Continents: Europe
by L. Foster
(Heinemann, 2003)

Immigrants from Eastern Europe
by Sarah Horrell
(Franklin Watts, 2003)

Hello, Europe! (Our Amazing Continents)
by April Pulley Sayre
(Millbrook Press, 2003)

World Organizations: European Union
by Jillian Powell
(Franklin Watts, 2004)

Useful addresses

Czech Centre London, 13 Harley Street, London W1G 9QG Tel: 020 7307 5180 Provides pamphlets and magazines about the Czech Republic, as well as maps and information.

Czech Embasssy, 26 Kensington Palace Gardens, London W8 4QY
Tel: 0207 243 1115

Sources

The statistics in this book are from the following sources:
CIA World Factbook
(www.cia.gov/cia/publications/factbook/)
City of Brno website (www.brno.cz)
United Nations Population Division
(www.un.org/esa/population/unpop.htm)
World Bank (www.worldbank.org)

The website addresses (URLs) included in this book were valid at the time of going to press. However, because of the nature of the Internet, it is possible that some addresses may have changed, or sites may have changed or closed down since publication. While the authors and publishers regret any inconvenience this may cause the readers, no responsibility for any such changes can be accepted by either the authors or the publisher.

Index

Page numbers in **bold** refer to photographs.